AMAZING
MIGRATIONS

SEA

Harriet Brundle

©2018
Book Life
King's Lynn
Norfolk PE30 4LS

ISBN: 978-1-78637-222-2

All rights reserved
Printed in Malaysia

Written by:
Harriet Brundle

Edited by:
Kirsty Holmes

Designed by:
Gareth Liddington

A catalogue record for this book
is available from the British Library.

AMAZING MIGRATIONS

CONTENTS

Words that look like **this** can be found in the glossary on page 24.

WHAT IS A HABITAT?

The place where an animal lives is called its habitat. A good habitat has food, water and a safe place for an animal to raise their **young**.

A Warm-Water Coral Reef

Although these fish all live in water, the temperature is different in each habitat.

A Cold-Water Stream

There are many types of habitat and each one is different.

Animals live in habitats that meet their needs. Some habitats meet the needs of lots of different animals so there will be many **species** living there.

6

SHARK

SEAWEED

FISH

Some habitats might have plants that animals use for food or shelter. Some animals eat other animals in their habitat to survive. This is called a food chain.

WHAT DOES MIGRATION MEAN?

Migration is the movement of animals from one place to another. Some animals move small distances when they migrate, while others travel hundreds of kilometres.

When animals migrate, they often stay together in groups for **protection** from other animals.

Fish need to watch out – some birds can grab them out of the water!

Animals often migrate to **breed** or lay eggs. Some species of crab migrate from deep water to shallow water to lay their eggs.

Some sea animals migrate to find more food or better **living conditions**. Many prefer warmer or cooler water at different times of the year.

SALMON

Most types of salmon are born in freshwater lakes. They migrate from the lakes to the sea to find food.

Salmon travel in groups called shoals.

After they have fed, salmon migrate back to the lakes to breed. To do so, they often have to travel **upstream**, jumping and diving to move upwards!

WHALES

Calf

Humpback Whale

Many species of whale migrate every year. They often find their food in cold water, but migrate to give birth in warmer water.

Humpback whales migrate nearly 5,000 kilometres. This is one of the longest migrations of any **mammal** on Earth.

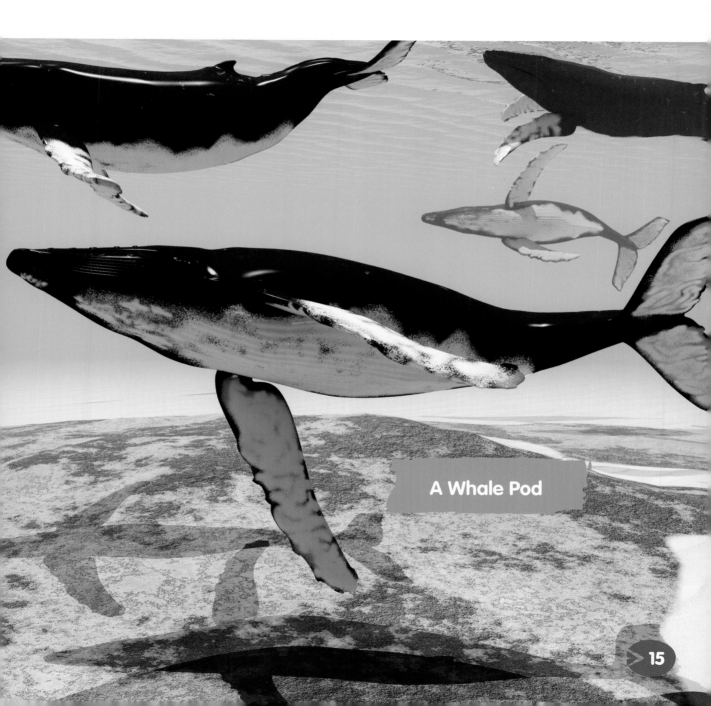

A Whale Pod

LEATHERBACK SEA TURTLES

Leatherback sea turtles migrate between areas with plenty of food and areas where they breed.

Leatherback sea turtles eat jellyfish and other soft-bodied sea creatures.

Leatherback sea turtles can migrate hundreds or even thousands of kilometres. One record-breaking turtle has been recorded as travelling over 19,000 kilometres!

THE SARDINE RUN

The sardine run is a migration of sardines that happens in South Africa, usually between the months of May and July.

Millions of sardines migrate each year!

Nobody is sure why the sardines migrate.

Birds, sharks and lots of other hungry animals feast on the shoals of sardines as they move.

The Earth is becoming hotter over time because of something known as climate change. Climate change is causing **weather patterns** to change.

Sea animals use the temperature of the ocean as a sign of when they should migrate. Climate change makes the sea warmer, so animals begin their journey at the wrong time.

1. Draw an 'under the sea' picture. How many different animals can you think of that live in the sea? Are they very big or very small?

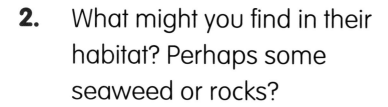

2. What might you find in their habitat? Perhaps some seaweed or rocks?

3. Add labels to your drawing to explain in more detail.

GLOSSARY

breed	to produce young
living conditions	the things that affect the way something lives
mammal	an animal that has warm blood, a backbone and produces milk
protection	looking after or keeping safe
shoal	a large group of the same type of fish
species	a group of very similar animals or plants that are able to produce young together
temperature	how hot a person, place or object is
upstream	moving against the flow of a river, towards its source
weather patterns	weather that we have become used to happening at particular times
young	an animal's offspring

INDEX